The Fulness of the Godhead

Michael Phelan

I0171005

ISBN: 978-1-78364-523-7

www.obt.org.uk

Unless indicated otherwise Scripture quotations are from The Authorized (King James) Version. Rights in the Authorized Version in the United Kingdom are vested in the Crown. Reproduced by permission of the Crown's patentee, Cambridge University Press.

****

The Open Bible Trust
Fordland Mount, Upper Basildon,
Reading, RG8 8LU, UK.

The Fulness

of the Godhead

Contents

INTRODUCTION

INTRODUCTION

This publication is offered to the reader in the prayerful hope that it will be of some benefit to those who wish to understand what the Bible says concerning the nature of the Lord Jesus Christ, and of the Holy Spirit, and of Their relationship to the Father. Throughout the history of the Christian Church, men have asked whether Christ is truly God, and whether the Holy Spirit is a real Person, or simply a Divine force. This is a modest attempt to provide the Bible's answers to these questions. May it be to the glory of God. It is my prayer that the words of the psalmist may be in the hearts and minds of all who read this, "Open Thou mine eyes, that I may behold wondrous things out of Thy Law," (Psalm 119:18). "Ask the God of our Lord Jesus Christ, the glorious Father, to give you the Spirit, Who will make you wise and reveal God to you, so that you will know Him," (Ephesians 1:17 *Good News Bible*).

Unless otherwise stated, all Biblical quotations are made from the *King James Authorized Version*. It should be pointed out that whenever the word *Divine* is used in this study, it is to be understood in its strongest form, meaning *absolute Deity*, not merely *godly,* or *God-like.*

THE UNION OF THE FATHER, SON, AND SPIRIT

THE UNION OF THE FATHER, SON, AND SPIRIT

It is beyond the ability of mere human words to describe the greatness of our God. Throughout the sacred scriptures we may find instances where the inspired writers have gone beyond the bounds of normal grammatical structure in order to convey to us the truths about God they wished us to understand. The Infinity That is God can never be tied down by words. It can only be praised and adored in true worship and veneration. The one thing we must avoid at all costs is submitting to the temptation to *cut down* God to our own size (Psalm 50:21b). He is above and beyond all that we may say or think about Him, (Isaiah 55:8-9).

A very good friend of mine used to tell me that my idea of God was not big enough; he would then add that neither was his, nor anybody else's for that matter! It is impossible for any man, equipped as we all are with a finite mind, and hence a limited understanding, to fully comprehend God. We must ensure, therefore, that we obtain the largest view possible of Him. Now, being Infinite and, therefore, Indefinable, any idea or conception which our intellects can formulate about God will be hopelessly inadequate. Bearing this in mind, how much more should we be on our guard against ideas and notions that tend to limit God, ideas that reduce Him in our minds. All such ideas will seriously undermine our Spiritual life.

A major part of a Christian's spiritual life is prayer, a matter with which God is mightily concerned, as we discover from Romans 8:26. There Paul tells us, "The Spirit helps us in our weakness; for we do not know how to pray as we ought, but the Spirit Himself intercedes for us with sighs too deep for words," (*R.S.V.*). God's interest in our prayers is so intense that the Holy Spirit makes *intercession* on our behalf to the Father, because "we know not what we should pray for as we ought," helping us in our clumsy and awkward attempts at prayer, interceding, "with groanings which cannot be uttered." It is all too easy to pass over that verse glibly without considering its tremendous implication; we would do well to meditate upon it humbly with awe and wonder.

The interceding role which the Holy Spirit fulfills on our behalf, "according to the will of God" (v.27), intimately links the Spirit with our Lord Jesus Christ as we see from Romans 8:34, and Hebrews 7:25, where the author of the epistle tells us that Jesus Christ's role in relation to the saints is one where, "He ever liveth to make *intercession* for them." Thus we see a *union* between the Spirit and Christ in performing the Will of the Father.

This union is also seen in the sphere of Creation. "In the beginning God created the heavens and the earth," declared Moses in Genesis 1:1. John the evangelist in the first chapter of his Gospel adds, "In the beginning was the Word, and the Word was with God, and the Word was God. The same was in the beginning with God. All things were made by Him; and without Him was not anything made that was made." John 1:1-3. This thought is echoed by Paul, in his epistle to the Colossians, "For by Him (Christ) were all things created, that are in heaven, and that are in earth, visible and invisible." Colossians 1:16. Here we see both Father and Son co-operative in the act of Creation, sharing together the wonderful birth of the heavens and the earth, yet they were not alone, the Spirit was there also as Moses recorded in Genesis 1:2, "And the Spirit of God moved upon the face of the waters." Elihu knew of the creativity of the Spirit when he said in Job 33:4, "The Spirit of God hath made me," as did Job himself when he affirmed, "By His Spirit He hath garnished the heavens," Job 26:13.

The Psalmist also may be called upon to testify in this respect. In Psalm 33:6 we read, "By the Word of the Lord were the heavens made; and all the host of them by the breath of Him mouth." Now here again we see Christ as the Word, operating in a Creative role, but our main interest here lies in the second part of the verse, "and all the host of them by the breath of His mouth," where I believe a more accurate rendering would read, "and all the host of them by the *Spirit* of His mouth."[1]

---

[1] Robert Young's *Analytical Concordance To The Holy Bible* shows that the word translated *Breath* in the A.V. is the Hebrew word *ruach*. Referring to his *Hebrew Index, Lexicon,* we see that, in the overwhelming majority of cases, *ruach* is translated *Spirit*. The statistics are:

Spirit	232 occurrences	
Wind	90	" "
Breath	28	" "
Various others	26	" "

Bearing in mind that *ruach* is most often taken to mean *Spirit,* and considering also the role of the Spirit in creation as evidenced by Genesis 1:2, Job 33:4, & 26:13, I believe that the correct rendering of Psalm 33:6 would be, "By the Word (Christ) of the Lord (The Father) were the heavens made; and all the host of them by the (Holy) Spirit of His mouth."

Thus we see established the Creativity of the Holy Spirit, and, as with the role of intercession, this is an activity which the Spirit shares with the Son, or Word of God, and more than this, it is an activity which both the Son and the Spirit share with the Father, which implies a Union of the closest and most intimate nature. This Union of the Father, the Son, and the Holy Spirit leads us to the famous passages in the book of Genesis, where the plural personal pronouns, *us* and *our* are applied to God. The passages in question are: Ch.1:26, "And God said, 'Let *US* make man in *OUR* Image, after *OUR* likeness.'" Ch.3:22, "And the Lord God said, "Behold, the man is become as *One of US,*'" Ch. 11:6-7, "And the Lord said...'Let *US* go down.'"[2] Having already seen that the Father, Son and Spirit were *all* active in the Creation, it is most reasonable to find that God says, "Let *US* make man in *OUR* Image, after *OUR* likeness." The obvious plurality of these pronouns confirms our previous findings regarding the Union of the Father, Son, and Spirit, but what does Scripture reveal to us about Their natures? It is accepted without contention that the Father is God, but what of the Spirit, and the Son? Who are they? Must we ascribe Deity to them, or, are they simply creations of the Father? Our next step must be to consider the Holy Spirit, and the Son of God, the Lord Jesus Christ, and ascertain what the Bible says about Them.[3]

---

[2] See also Isaiah 6:8, "Also I heard the voice of the Lord, saying, "Whom shall I send, and who will go for *Us*?"

[3] A view that I am not at all unsympathetic to is that further evidence for the Union of Father, Son and Spirit is to be found in the Hebrew Name for God, *Elohim*. For a discussion on this matter please refer to *Appendix 1*.

THE HOLY SPIRIT

THE HOLY SPIRIT

We have seen how the Holy Spirit, along with the Word, was active in the Creation, together with the Father, a fact that has led many to conclude that the Godhead comprises more than one Person. However, there are many sincere people, who are earnestly seeking for the Truth who believe, or have been taught that, not only is the Holy Spirit *not* a Personality of the Godhead, but that the Holy Spirit has no Personality at all.

Now what are we to make of this? Here, we have two views that are totally opposed. One is that the Holy Spirit is a mighty Person of the Godhead, worthy of our highest acts of admiration and praise, and the other is that the Holy Spirit is but a kind of created force, totally void of personality, even, of life itself. A greater difference of belief would not be possible. Ours is the task of establishing which is the truth. One particular view may appeal to us as seeming more noble than the other, but of course, we need far more than mere feelings to go on. To know the Truth we must call upon the Lord to be our guide, we must call upon His help because we cannot "search out" God for ourselves, (Job 11:7). However, God can and does reveal Himself to us by means of prayer, and by the study of His Word.

We have already seen that the usual Hebrew word for *spirit, ruach,* means *breath*. A similar situation applies to the New Testament. In the *Authorised Version* there are only two Greek words used throughout the New Testament for *spirit,* namely, *phantasma,* which is used only twice, in Matthew 14:26, and Mark 6:49, and is in each case more accurately rendered *ghost*, as in *Revised Standard Version*, and *pneuma*, which again means *breath*.[4]

We must ask ourselves that is meant by this continuous use of the word, *breath* in both Testaments, to signify the Holy Spirit? Could it ne that in the very word itself lies one of the answers to the questions about the nature of God's Spirit that we are seeking? Could it be that God is showing us that as breath is the very Hall-mark of life, His Spirit is alive? As breath presupposes life, it seems difficult to believe that the symbol of breath could signify a non-living force. Further, it was the breath of God's mouth which turned the earthly body of Adam into a living person (Genesis 2:7). We may conclude, therefore, that God's breath, or Spirit, contained all that was necessary to impart life, and personality to Adam, a fact that encourages us to believe that the Spirit, too, is alive and personal.[5]

It would appear from the words of Christ in John's Gospel, that there is no other view open to us. The words of Christ are the ultimate authority for all who call upon His Name, it is the will of God that we listen to them (Matthew 17:5), they are the bedrock of

---

[4] See Robert Young's *Analytical Concordance To The Holy Bible,* or James Strong's *Exhaustive Concordance Of The Bible,* or word No. 4151 in Thayer's *Greek Lexicon,* also W.E. Vine's *Expository Dictionary Of New Testament Words.*

[5] Note also the Spirit's role in the Incarnation of Christ Jesus the Lord, Whom Scripture declares to be the Last Adam, (1 Corinthians 15:45). The Bible shows that the conception of Jesus in Mary's womb was accomplished by the Holy Spirit coming upon Mary, again illustrating His creative and life-giving ability, (Luke 1:35).

our faith. In John 14:6, He declares, "*I* am …the Truth." It is, therefore, a very grave matter to disbelieve His words. Whatever our blessed Lord Jesus Christ has to say about any issue, we must regard as being conclusive; let us then examine His statements about the Holy Spirit, and see what we may learn from them.

It is noteworthy that in the Gospel of John, Christ repeatedly speaks of the Holy Spirit, as being a Person. What especially draws our attention to this, is that it defies the normal rules of grammar. The Greek word for *Spirit, pneuma,* is neuter, the Aramaic *rucha* (equivalent to the Hebrew *ruach*), the word the Lord would actually have spoken, is feminine, yet the Lord deliberately and persistently referred to the Holy Spirit in *masculine* terms.[6]

The Lord Jesus Christ said, "But the Comforter, which is The Holy Ghost, Whom the Father will send in My Name, *HE* shall teach you all things," (John 14:26). "But when the Comforter is come, *WHOM* I will send unto you from the Father, even The Spirit Of Truth, which proceedeth from the Father, *HE* shall testify of Me," (John 15:26). "I will send *HIM* (The Comforter) unto you. And when *HE* is come, He will reprove the world of sin," (John 16:7,8). "Howbeit when *HE*, The Spirit of Truth, is come, *HE* will guide you into all Truth; for *HE* shall not speak of *HIMSELF*; but whatsoever *HE* shall hear, that shall *HE* speak: and *HE* will shew you things to come. *HE* shall glorify Me; for *HE* shall receive of Mine, and shall shew it unto you," (John 16:13-14).

The words of Leon Morris on this issue are most helpful. He says, "Now in Greek the word for *Spirit* is neuter, and should in strict grammar be referred to as *It*. When John uses a pronoun to refer to

---

[6] See W.E. Vine op. cit. page 64, Vol. IV.

Spirit and the two words are close together, he usually respects his grammar and uses the correct form *It*. But if a word or two intervenes he nearly always uses the masculine form *He*. This is grammatically incorrect, but most illuminating. The explanation is surely that John habitually thought of the Spirit in personal terms, as *He* rather than as *It*. Naturally enough his thinking dictated this form of speech. Where he can, he uses personal forms of the pronouns. He even does it occasionally where the pronoun and the word for Spirit occur side by side. See John 16:13, 'he, the Spirit of truth'."[7]

There are those who account for the masculine pronouns by saying that instead of referring to the word for *Spirit*, they refer to the word for *Comforter*, which is masculine in the original Greek. However, the question then arises, 'Why did John select a word which is unmistakably masculine to describe the *neuter 'Spirit'* if the Holy Spirit is not a masculine Person?'

There are others who urge us to believe that the Lord is speaking metaphorically here. The danger of this argument is that it permits us to make the Scriptures say whatever we ourselves wish them to, a practice Peter warns us about, (2 Peter 3:16). A justifiable reason

---

[7] *Spirit Of The Living God,* by Leon Morris, page 36, published by Inter-Varsity Press. See also, *The Trinity* by Edward Henry Bickersteth, page 126, published by Kregel Publications; *What The Bible Teaches,* by R.A. Torrey, page 226, published by Oliphants; *The Creeds: Their History, Nature and Use,* by Harold Smith, M.A., page 121, published by Robert Scott; *Systematic Theology* by A.H. Strong, page 323, published by Pickering & Inglis. Note also that Tischendorf along with some others translates Ephesians 1:14, "*Who* is an earnest of our inheritance."

must first be found before the clear and literal meaning of any verse of Scripture is discarded for a more obscure interpretation. It is my belief that no such reason may in this case be produced.

Again in the Gospel of John, the Lord Jesus names the Holy Spirit, *The Comforter.* The original Greek word is *parakletos,* and this gives us further help concerning the Spirit's Personality, for besides meaning *comforter,* or *consoler* it also means *one who stands by,* or *advocate*[8], roles which it is difficult to imagine a mere force fulfilling. Christ, by calling the Holy Spirit *another Parakletos* in John 14:16, is comparing the Spirit to Himself, for *parakletos*, as we have noted, means *advocate*, and Christ Himself is called our *Advocate* in John 2:1, "And if any man sin, we have an *ADVOCATE* (Greek: *parakletos.*) with the Father, Jesus Christ the righteous."[9]

---

[8] See W.E. Vine, op. cit., page 208, Vol. 1 & word No. 3875 in Thayer's op. cit.

[9] Leon Morris notes that, "In Greek there are two words for *other*: *allos* means another of the same kind, while *heteros* points rather to *another of a different kind.* Thus if I ask for another book, using *allos,* I am seeking another copy of the volume in question. But if you bring me a copy of another book altogether I might complain that I didn't say *heteros.* When Jesus speaks of the Spirit as *"another Comforter"* (John 14:16) the word He uses is *allos.* The most natural interpretation of all this is that the Spirit is to be thought of as another like Jesus. As Jesus is a Person, the inference is that the Spirit is also a Person. The only catch in the reasoning is that not all Greek writers used the two words for *other* strictly. Some did; some did not. It is not completely certain that John did (he uses *heteros* so rarely that we cannot be sure). But as far as it

Now the role of an Advocate is to *intercede*. We have already seen that both the Spirit and the Word act as our Intercessors, by the words of Romans 8:26 & 34, and Hebrews 7:25, (see above). These, of course, are roles which may only be undertaken by *real persons*. Just as Jesus Christ *must* be a real Person in order to be our Advocate, and Intercessor, so must the Holy Spirit, whom Scripture presents as our other Advocate and Intercessor, be a *real Person*. An impersonal force cannot speak on our behalf, or *intercede* for us to the Father. An impersonal force could never *come alongside* us, to be our Advocate with God. An impersonal force cannot ever be compared with our Living, Loving, Risen Saviour.

This, however, is but half the story. There are many other attributes of the Holy Spirit, which illustrate His Personality, as the following examples show. The Holy Spirit is said to search, "For the Spirit *searcheth* all things," 1 Corinthians 2:10; and to possess knowledge, "The things of God knoweth no man, but the Spirit of God," 1 Corinthians 2:11; and to have a mind, "For *it seemed good* to the Holy Ghost," Acts 15:28; "He that searcheth the hearts knoweth what is *the mind of the Spirit*," Romans 8:27; "But all these worketh that one and the Selfsame Spirit, dividing to every man severally *as HE will*," 1 Corinthians 12:11; and, sadly, may be grieved, "Grieve not the Holy Spirit of God," Ephesians 4:30.

The Holy Spirit speaks, "The Spirit of the Lord spoke to me," 2 Samuel 23:2; "It is not ye that speak, but the Holy Ghost," Mark 13:11; "*The Holy Ghost said,* 'Separate *ME* Barnabus and Saul for the work whereunto *I* have called them,'" Acts 13:2; "*Thus saith*

---

goes the point is valid. The most natural way of understanding *another* is 'another of like kind'." Op. cit., page 36.

the Holy Ghost," Acts 21:11; "*Well spake the Holy Ghost,*" Acts 28:25; "Now the Spirit *speaketh expressly,*" 1 Timothy 4:1; "He that hath as ear, *let him hear what the Spirit saith,*" Revelation 2:7. The Holy Spirit is our Teacher, "Thou gavest also Thy Good Spirit to *instruct* them," Nehemiah 9:20; "The Holy Ghost … shall *teach* you all things," John 14:26. He gives us commands, "So they, *being sent forth by the Holy Ghost,*" Acts 13:4; "They…were *forbidden* of the Holy Ghost … The Spirit *suffered them not,*" Acts 16:6-7. It is possible to lie to the Holy Spirit, "Why hath Satan filled thine heart to *lie* to the Holy Ghost," Acts 5:3. The Holy Spirit reveals to us, "It was *revealed* unto him by the Holy Ghost," Luke 2:26; "*HE* (The Spirit)…will shew you things to come," John 16:13; "God hath revealed them unto us by His Spirit," 1 Corinthians 2:10.

In addition to this, the Holy Spirit is said to *dwell*, that is *live,* in the hearts of believers. In Romans 8:9, the word Paul uses for the indwelling of the Holy Spirit is the Greek word, *oikeo* which is also used to denote the way in which a husband and wife live together in the same home, such is the nearness and loveliness of the indwelling or *inliving* of the Spirit of God in the lives of His children.[10]

Wonderful and glorious though this experience undeniably is, Paul actually surpasses it when he says in 1 Corinthians 6:19, "Know ye not that your body is the *Temple* of the Holy Ghost." Here, we are taken far beyond mere acknowledgement of the Personality of God's Spirit of Truth, to a place where we must bow our knees, and bow our hearts, and confess nothing less than the Spirit's Deity. A

---

[10] See W.E. Vine, op. cit., page 344, Vol. 1 & word No. 3611 in Thayer's op. cit.

dwelling is a place where any person may reside, but a Temple is Holy ground, the sacred and hallowed place, where the Presence of our God is to be found! Seeking evidence of the Spirit's Personality has brought us face to face with His Godhood!

Let us see if there is anything else in the Word of God which shows the Godhood of the Holy Spirit. The *creativity* of the Spirit has already been noted, now *creation* is a prerogative of the Deity alone. Men, or angels, or any mere creature, can only re-arrange pre-existing materials. Whatever mankind produces, whether it be the Space Shuttle Craft, or the Mona Lisa, the pyramids, or a ball point pen, constitutes only a working of raw material. God alone can create that material, and hence, any Person Who is said to be capable of real creativity, must be of the Godhead.

In Hebrews 9:14 the Holy Spirit is said to be *Eternal*; Psalm 139:7-10 shows us the *Omnipresence* of the Spirit; John 14:26, 16:12,13, and 1 Corinthians 2:10-11 display His *Omniscience*; and John 6:63 and 1 Peter 3:18B reveal that the Holy Spirit is the *Author of Life*. In the light of all these Scriptures how can we deny the Deity of God's Holy Spirit? These facts alone are sufficient for us to conclude that the Holy Spirit is a vital Personality of the Godhead, indeed, even if there was no further revelation concerning the subject, this would be the only satisfactory conclusion to draw. But now, if we press on, we will see that this is a truth that is not merely *implied* by certain texts, but that the Scriptures *explicitly* speak of the Holy Spirit as being Divine.

In Isaiah 6:8-10, we find the following, "Also I heard the voice of the Lord, saying, 'Whom shall *I* send, and who will go for Us?' Then said I, 'Here am I; send me,' And He said, 'Go, and tell this people, "Hear ye indeed, but understand not; and see ye indeed, but perceive not. Make the heart of this people fat, and make their ears heavy, and shut their eyes; lest they see with their eyes, and hear with their ears, and understand with their heart, and convert, and be healed."'" Now, this we are told, is the Lord God HimSelf speaking, however, Paul, when he quotes this passage of Isaiah in Acts 28:25-27 ascribes these very words to the Holy Spirit, saying "Well spake the *Holy Ghost* by *Esias* the prophet unto our fathers." *Adonay,* the name for God in Isaiah 6:8, which is rendered *Lord* in the Authorized Version, is applied by Paul to the Holy Spirit, making Him *Lord* also.

If we turn to Psalm 95:8-11, we read of the rebellion of Israel in the desert in these words, "Harden not your heart, as in the provocation, and as in the day of temptation in the wilderness; when your fathers tempted Me, proved Me, and saw My work. Forty years long was *I* grieved with this generation, and said, 'It is a people that do err in their heart, and they have not known My ways:' unto whom I sware in My wrath that they should not enter into My rest." It is quite evident from the personal pronouns, *I, Me,* and *My,* that it is God Himself Who is the Speaker here, and verses 6-7 confirm this, "...The Lord (*Yahweh*) our Maker...He is our God...Hear His voice..." Significantly, when this passage is quoted in the New Testament, in Hebrews 3:7-11 as before, the words are attributed to the Holy Spirit, "Wherefore *as the Holy Ghost saith,* 'Today if ye will hear His voice, Harden not you hearts, as in the provocation, in the day of temptation in the wilderness'" et cetera. Here the Holy Spirit is irrefutably shown to be of the Godhead. The Divine Name, *Yahweh,* or *Jehovah* that is rendered *Lord* in the Authorized Version of Psalm 95, is applied by the writer to the Hebrews, to the Holy Spirit HimSelf, making Him also *Yahweh,* or *Jehovah,* that is *Self-Existent* or *The Eternal One,* and therefore Divine.

Now, this is not the only time that the Holy Spirit is referred to as *Yahweh* or *Jehovah*. In Exodus 34:34, we read of the veil that Moses wore over his face, "But when Moses went in before the Lord (*Yahweh*) to speak with Him, he took the veil off, until he came out." When Paul refers to this verse in 2 Corinthians 3:17, he calls the *Lord* in this passage, the Spirit! "Now the Lord (*Yahweh*) is that Spirit", or, as the *Good News Bible* puts it, "Now 'the Lord,' in this passage *is the Spirit*"!

The fact that the Holy Spirit is named *The Lord* in Scripture should not surprise us, considering the words of Christ in John 4:24, "God *is* Spirit."[11] Further, how could the blasphemy against the Holy Spirit ever be the one unforgivable sin, if He was not Very God HimSelf? Could it ever be that it is forgivable to blaspheme God, but *un*forgivable to blaspheme one of His creations? Matthew 12:31-32 says, "All manner of sin and blasphemy shall be forgiven unto men: *but the blasphemy against the Holy Ghost shall not be forgiven unto men.* And whosoever speaketh a word against the Son of Man, it shall be forgiven him: *But whosoever speaketh against the Holy Ghost, it shall not be forgiven him, neither in this world, neither in the world to come"*. Little wonder that Peter told Ananias that, in lying to the Holy Spirit, he was lying to God HimSelf, Acts 5:3-4.

---

[11] There is no indefinite article in Greek, which means this verse may either be read as 'God is *a* Spirit', as in the *A.V.*, or *'God is Spirit'*, as in the *R.S.V., James Moffat, Good News Bible, N.I.V., Living Bible, J.B. Phillips, & The New Testament In Basic English.* This to my mind is far better, as the former rendering makes God merely *a* Spirit among many others.

We have seen then, how the Scriptures clearly show us not only the Personality of the Holy Spirit, and the wonderful works that He does for all believers, but also His Divine Majesty, which is to be worshipped and adored by us. Let us give thanks to the Lord, for the Comforter that He has sent!

THE LORD JESUS CHRIST

THE LORD JESUS CHRIST

We must turn now from the Spirit, to the Word of God, Who, as God's Annointed, the Messiah of the Old Testament, and the Christ of the New, became manifest in human form as *Emmanuel, God-With-Us,* and was named *Jesus.* [12] As such, He is the Mediator of the New Covenant, or Testament, between God and man, (1 Timothy 2:5), the Means of our Redemption, the Only Hope of all mankind. "Neither is there salvation in any other (than Christ): for there is none other Name under heaven given among men, *whereby we must be saved,*" Acts 4:12. "I (Jesus) am the resurrection and the life; he that believeth in Me, though he were dead, *yet shall he live,*" John 11:25.

These, and many other Scriptures, show how absolutely dependent we are for our salvation on the Lord Jesus Christ, and how all our hopes center on Him, and on Him alone. He is the *Door* or *Way* to the Father, "I (Christ) am the Way ... no man cometh unto the Father, but by Me," John 14:6. To believe then, that the Lord Jesus Christ is less than God, that He is a *created* being, is to make us dependent upon, and worshipful of, a mere *creature*, rather than God HimSelf. The seriousness of this is made clear to us by Romans 1:25, where Paul talking of the unsaved says, "(They) changed the Truth of God into a lie, and worshipped and served the *creature* more than the *Creator*, Who is blessed for ever."

---

[12] *Jesus* is derived from the Greek form of *Jeshua,* which is itself derived from *Joshua,* and means *Jehovah-is-salvation.*

Now the Lord Jesus Christ *is* the Creator, together with the Father and the Spirit; the whole of the creation was brought forth by Him, from the vast galaxies of stars, to the least blade of grass. "By the Word (Christ) of the Lord were the heavens made," Psalm 33:6. "All things were made by Him (Christ); and without Him was not anything made that was made," John 1:3. "For by Him (Christ) were all things created, that are in heaven, and that are in earth, visible and invisible, whether they be thrones, or dominions, or principalities, or powers: all things were created by Him, and for Him," Colossians 1:16, (cf. Hebrews 1:2, 2:10, & 11:3).

Thus, Christ is seen to be the very Lord of all creation, the Architect, Builder, and Sustainer of the universe, and, as with the Father and the Spirit, He is also the Source, and Giver of Life, for John notes that, "In Him (Christ) was Life," John 1:4. His life is not dependent on anyone or anything else, as ours is, being mere creatures. He is *Self-Sustaining* or *Self-Existent* (the meaning of the Name *Yahweh*,[13] and therefore Divine. "Life was *in* Him," and flowed *out* of Him to give life to others. He was, and is, the Fountainhead of life, all else is dependent on Him, (c.f. Colossians 1:17).

In order to create all things in the Beginning, Christ must have existed *before* the Beginning, before the existence of time, space, and matter, when there was only God. In John 17:5, Christ remembers the glory He had before the creation thus, "And now, O Father, glorify Thou Me with Thine Own Self with the glory which *I* had with Thee *before* the *Kosmos* (Greek) was." Paul, in Colossians 1:17 says, "He (Christ) is *before* all things," The

---

[13] A.H. Strong, *Systematic Theology,* page 257, published by Pickering & Inglis.

prophet Micah adds his testimony in Micah 5:2, "But thou, Bethlehem Ephratah, though thou be little among the thousands of Judah, yet out of thee shall He (Christ) come forth unto Me that is to be Ruler in Israel; Whose goings forth have been from of old, from the days of *eternity*," (margin). Thus we see Christ in the Beginning, and before the Beginning, which reminds us of the words of the writer to the Hebrews, who in Hebrews 7:3 says that one of the characteristics of Christ is *"before all ages"* (*N.I.V.*), or as the *R.S.V.,* and *James Moffat* express the same verse, He is *"before all time."* I believe that this can only be regarded as evidence for the Deity of Christ.

If we deny the Deity of Christ, we find ourselves faced with the problem of how to explain the worship He received. The Lord Jesus Christ was worshipped even as a child, as Matthew records, by the Magi, or wise men, "And when they were come into the house, they saw the young Child with Mary His mother, and fell down, and *worshipped* Him,' Matthew 2:11. That this worship of the Lord Jesus by the Magi was legitimate, is obvious by the fact that they were led to Judea for that very purpose, by the sign ordained by God, the star spoken of in Numbers 24:17, "There shall come a Star out of Jacob, and a Sceptre shall rise out of Israel," and by God's Providential dealings with them, in leading them to Christ, and warning them to avoid Herod.

In view of all this, the worship they offered the Lord Jesus must have been acceptable to God and, as such, we may take it as an example for ourselves. Of course, to the Christian, who believes that the Lord Jesus Christ is a vital Personality of the Godhead, the worship of Christ contains no difficulties, but if we maintain that Christ is a *created* being, however exalted, it presents us with a dilemma. Paul, in Romans 1:25, proscribes the worship of any creature, and John was twice reprimanded for attempting to offer worship to a mere creature in Revelation 19:10 and 22:8-9, (cf. Acts 10:25-26). In the words of Jesus, as He addressed Satan, the author of false worship, and counterfeit religion, "Thou shalt worship the Lord thy God, and Him only shalt thou serve," Matthew 4:10.

Now, that Jesus Christ should utter these words, and then HimSelf accept worship on many different occasions, leads inevitably to the conclusion that Jesus is truly Divine, or else He would be a hypocrite. We are frequently told in the Gospels of instances where Christ was worshipped, and this worship was accepted by Him. But, if Christ was not Divine, and was therefore *unworthy* to receive adoration, He would have rejected this worship, not wishing to set such a bad example to other creatures.[14] However, not only do we have the accounts of the evangelists concerning Christ receiving worship, we also have the *command* of God to the angels to worship Him, "Let all the angels of God *worship* Him," Hebrews 1:6, Paul, in Philippians 2:10-11, says that "At the Name of Jesus *every knee should bow*, of things in heaven, and things on earth, and things under the earth: and that every tongue should confess that Jesus Christ is Lord, to the glory of God the Father."[15] The Father would have all His creatures honour the Son, *as they should honour HimSelf,* John 5:23.[16]

---

[14] For example see, Matthew 8:2, 9:18, 14:33, 15:25, 20:20, 28:9, 28:17; Mark 5:6; Luke 24:52; John 9:38.

[15] For the significance of the expression, *Jesus is Lord*, see Appendix 2.

[16] Paul writes in Philippians 2:10-11, "That at the Name of Jesus every knee should bow, and that every tongue should confess that Jesus Christ is Lord". It seems that Paul is referring here to Isaiah

It is sometimes suggested that because the Lord Jesus Christ is referred to as the *Son* of God, He must be *inferior* to the Father. While there does appear to be an established order of the Personalities comprising the Godhead, inasmuch as it is usual to refer to Them in the order of the Father, Son, and the Holy Spirit, as in Matthew 28:19, when Christ is called the *Son* of God, does it really imply inferiority? We know that, "That which is born of the flesh *is* flesh; and that which is born of the Spirit *is* spirit," John 3:6. Extending this thought a little, would it not follow that, 'that which is born (or begotten) of God, is God?' Certainly the Jews thought so, for when Christ said that God was His Father, the conclusion they immediately reached was that Jesus was making HimSelf *equal* with the Father! "Therefore the Jews sought the more to kill Him, because He not only had broken the Sabbath, *but*

45:21-24, "I the Lord (*Jehovah*)…there is no God else beside Me, a just God and a *Saviour;* there is none beside Me, Look unto Me, and be ye saved, (cf John 3:14-15 & Numbers 21:8-9), all the ends of the earth: for I am God, and there is none else. I have sworn by MySelf, the word is gone out of My mouth in righteousness, and shall not return. *That unto Me every knee shall bow, every tongue shall swear.* Surely, shall one say, in the Lord (*Jehovah*) have I righteousness (cf. 2 Corinthians 5:12) and strength, (cf Philippians 4:13): even to Him shall men come (cf. John 12:32): and all that are incensed against Him shall be ashamed," (cf. 1 Peter 2:8). By comparing all the many parallels with the New Testament in this passage of Isaiah, especially, "a Saviour: there is none beside Me" with "there is none other Name (than Christ's)…Whereby we must be saved," (Acts 4:12), it is seen that the One Whom Isaiah names *Jehovah* in these verses, is the One Paul calls Jesus in Philippians 2, displaying His Deity in verses 6, & 9-11.

said also that God was His Father, making HimSelf equal with God," John 5:18.

Now the Jews were right, for, Christ "Being in the Form of God, thought it *not robbery to be equal* with God," (Philippians 2:6). The Jews had this brought home to them on the occasion that Jesus told a sick man that his sins were forgiven, (Mark 2:1-12 cf Luke 7:48). The Jews, while misunderstanding Who Jesus was, knew that this was a claim to Deity, for they said to themselves, "Why doth this man thus speak blasphemies? Who can forgive sins but God only?" (Mark 2:7). While being mistaken over the identity of Jesus, these men obviously knew the Scriptures, for in this case they were right, no one but God may forgive sins, as all sin is rebellion against God; (see Micah 7:18, Psalm 130:4, & Isaiah 43:25).

Jesus, realizing they appreciated just what His words meant, continued, "Whether is it easier to say to the sick of the palsy, 'Thy sins be forgiven thee;' or to say, 'Arise, and take up thy bed and walk? But that ye may know that the Son of Man hath power on earth to forgive sins …I say unto thee (the sick man), Arise, and take up thy bed, and go thy way into thine house.'" (Mark 2:9-11).

Jesus now backs up His claim, with something not so easily dismissed. The indignant Jews witness a miracle of healing, by the One they have just accused of being a blasphemer! Christ compels them to take His claim seriously. He wrought this mighty act so "that ye may *know* that the Son of Man hath power on earth to forgive sins." That Jesus could cleanse a man inwardly, from sin. The implication was obvious. Christ had claimed full Divinity, and this angered the Jews, especially as the sick man's cure had endorsed that claim.

The Jews were surprised at Christ's claims to Divinity, yet their own Scriptures spoke of a Divine Messiah, "For unto us a Child is born, into us a Son is given; and the government shall be upon His shoulder; and His Name shall be called 'Wonderful,' 'Counsellor,' *'The Mighty God,'* 'The Everlasting Father,' 'The Prince of Peace,' " (Isaiah 9:6). As only one Member of the Godhead is referred to in this passage, the singular Name for God, *El,* is used, from which derives *Eloah,* the singular form of the plural *Elohim.* However, it is coupled with the adjective *gibbor* translated *mighty* to emphasize the power and Godhead of that Son, the same word being found in Deuteronomy 10:17, where Jehovah is described as being *gibbor* or, as it is again rendered, *mighty.*[17] Thus, we see why Isaiah when speaking of the same Son in chapter 7, verse 14, names Him, *God-with-us,'* "Behold, a virgin shall conceive, and bear a Son, and shall

---

[17] See *The Exhaustive Concordance Of The Bible,* by James Strong. The title *The Everlasting Father* has more than one possible meaning. Some would render it as "The Father (Originator) of The Ages". Bickersteth favors "The Father of Eternity", (*The Trinity,* page 32, Kregel Publications). Gesenius believes that this phrase shows that the Messiah is the "Eternal Father of the people", inasmuch as He is a "bringer up" or "nourisher", "bestowing His benefits like a parent." He suggests the expression "Perpetual Father" signifying the "perpetuity of time" indicated to him by the word '*ad.* (See his *Hebrew Chaldee Lexicon* under the word Nos. 1 & 5703.) This is a view A.H. Strong would seem to hold, as he states that this verse is to be understood as attributing *eternity* to Christ. He says further, that "because Christ is the Source of all spiritual life for His people, He is called, in Is. 9:6 'Everlasting Father', and it is said in Is. 53:10, that 'He shall see His seed.'" (*Systematic Theology,* pages 310 & 797, Pickering & Inglis) cf. "The *children* which God hath given Me (Christ)," (Hebrews 2:13).

call His Name Immanuel." (That is, 'God-with-us', see Matthew 1:22-23.)

The Word of God, a vital Person of the Godhead, would become flesh, and dwell among ordinary men and women of the world, (John 1:14). Christ entered the world, and became man, yet in Him dwelt, *"all the fullness of the Godhead bodily,"* Colossians 2:9. Hence Christ's claims to Divinity, and His continued exercise of Divine power, particularly in His miracles of healing,[18] and His conquest over the grave.

---

[18] One of the most interesting instances of Christ's healing ministry is recounted in chapter 9 of John's Gospel, where a man, blind from birth, was given his sight by the Lord Jesus. Christ first made mud from the ground under their feet, and then anointed the man's eyes with this mud. After washing, the man was able to see. He had been healed! It has been suggested that the Lord adopted this method of healing to demonstrate that He was the One Who had formed not only Adam's eyes, but his whole body from the dust of the ground. If Christ did indeed form two new eyes from the mud, or clay as the A.V. calls it, it is an intriguing piece of evidence for the Deity of Christ, for the creation of Adam from :the dust of the ground" is ascribed in Genesis 2:7 to *Jehovah* Elohim. (cf John 1:1-3 where every item of creation is said to have been formed by the Word. Therefore, the Word is Jehovah Elohim!) After the body of Adam had been thus formed, Jehovah Elohim made Adam "a living soul" by breathing into his nostrils, "the breath of life." We have already seen that the breath of God's mouth is the Holy Spirit, (cf John 6:63 "It is the Spirit that gives life." *R.S.V.*). However, in John 20:22, Christ performs a similar act, "And when He (Christ) had said this, He *breathed* on them, (the disciples), and saith unto them, 'Receive

It was after this stupendous victory over death that Thomas made his famous declaration in John 20:28. Confronted by the Living Christ, Thomas doubts no longer, and in renewal of faith hails Jesus as, "*My Lord and my God.*" The words of Thomas here are clear and unambiguous. He calls Christ by the very name of Deity, '*Ho Theos,*' and Jesus does *not* rebuke him! Instead, Christ *accepts* his worship, and in accepting it, accepts also the title bestowed upon Him. Considering this in the light of Paul's words in Philippians 2:9, where he states that Christ has, "A Name which is above every name," (a description which only the Name of *God* fulfills) I can only conclude that Jesus Christ is truly God.

It has been suggested that Thomas used the Name of God to express his astonishment at the Miracle of the Resurrection. But, how can this be held without charging Thomas with grievously breaking the Lord's commands? (Exodus 20:7, cf Matthew 5:33-36, James 5:12.) Further, if this *was* the case, would not the Lord have immediately corrected him? I believe, rather, that this is an instance where the Son has been honored, even as the Father is honored (John 5:23) Who is HimSelf referred to as '*Ho Theos.*' (e.g. 2 Corinthians 1:3), showing the equality of Father and Son.

This view in reinforced by the words of Paul, in Romans 9:5, where he says that Christ is, "*Over all, God blessed for ever,*" and again in Titus 2:13, where he affirms Christians must look for, "The glorious appearing of the *great God* and our Saviour Jesus Christ." Notice that Jesus Christ is here called the *Great God!* To postulate two different Persons in this verse, One called the *Great God,* and

ye the Holy Ghost.'" This parallel encourages the belief that Jehovah and Christ are the same Person.

the other being Jesus Christ, is to beset ourselves with difficulties.[19] Consider that it is the *Great God* Who is said to *gloriously appear*. Now, Whose *glorious appearing* is it that Christians look for?

Unquestionably, we look for the *glorious appearing* of our Lord and Saviour Jesus Christ! Matthew 24:30, "Then shall *appear* the sign of the Son of Man in heaven …They shall see the Son of Man coming in the clouds of heaven with power and *great glory*.: Chapter 25: verse 31, "The Son of Man shall come in His *glory* and all the holy angels with Him, then shall He sit upon the throne of His *glory*." 1 Timothy 6:14, "Keep this commandment … until the *appearing* of our Lord Jesus Christ." 2 Timothy 4:1, "The Lord Jesus Christ … shall judge the quick and the dead at His *appearing* and His kingdom," (cf Revelation 19:11-16). This *glorious appearing* can only be the Second Coming of Christ to reign *gloriously* over the earth. Nowhere does the Bible say that we must look for the Father to appear, indeed the Bible shows us that He is invisible,"(Christ) is the *Image* (Appearance) of the *Invisible God*," (Colossians 1:15). The Father is unseen, but is revealed in and through the Son, (John 1:18). The "Great God" of Titus 2:13, who is said to *gloriously appear* can be none other than the Lord Jesus.

The light shed by these Scriptures illuminates the words of Luke, in Acts 20:28, where he calls upon the Overseers to "Feed the Church of God, which He (God) hath purchased with His Own blood." Now, it is of course, the blood of the Lamb, Christ Jesus,

---

[19] Alan G. Nute notes that "the presence of only one definite article … has the effect of binding together the two titles, (God, and Saviour)," See *A New Testament Commentary* edited by G.C.D. Howley, F.F. Bruce, & H.L. Ellison, page 528, published by Pickering & Inglis.

shed at Calvary, that is the price of the redemption of the saints, yet here significantly, Luke calls the blood of the Lamb, the blood of God.

This situation is found again in Zechariah chapter 12. Referring first to verses 1 and 4, it will be seen that it is the Lord, Jehovah, Who is the Speaker, "The word of the Lord for Israel, saith the Lord, (Jehovah)," (verse 1). "In that day, saith the Lord (Jehovah)", (verse 4). Then, if we move on, we come to these words in verse 10, "They shall look upon ME Whom they have pierced," This verse looks forward to the Crucifixion, as John the Evangelist shows in John 19:37, where he quotes this very verse from the book of Zechariah, and applies it, under Divine Inspiration, to the Passion of Christ. Jehovah, the Lord, is the Speaker in these verses, as we have seen, and He states "They shall look upon ME (Who is shown by John 19:37 to be Christ) Whom they have pierced." Clearly Jesus HimSelf is Jehovah, the Lord in Whom dwelt," all the fullness of the Godhead bodily," Colossians 2:9; Who is *Immanuel,*(God-with-us), Isaiah 7:14; the Promised Son, Who is called "The Mighty God," in Isaiah 9:6, the One Whom Jeremiah names, "The Lord (Jehovah) Our Righteousness," Jeremiah 23:6. Small wonder that the writers of the New Testament consistently refer to Him as God.

While on the Isle of Patmos, John received a vision of the Lord Jesus Christ, which fully revealed His Deity.[20] Hearing a mighty

---

[20] It would be helpful to the reader to have his or her Bible open at Revelation chapter 1, while reading this section. I have followed the Received Text here, which includes the phrase, "I am Alpha and Omega" in verse 11, which Westcott and Hort does not. Chapter 22, verses 13 & 16, show Christ naming HimSelf, 'Alpha

voice behind him, John had turned around to see Who was the Speaker, and was then confronted by the glorified Christ, the very *Express Image* of God, (Hebrews 1:3 cf Colossians 1:15). Such was the glory of Jesus, that John's senses were completely overpowered, and he collapsed, rendered unconscious by the sheer brilliance of Christ's appearance, (cf 2 Thessalonians 2:8 end). John wrote, "And when I saw Him (Christ), I fell at His feet as dead. And He laid His right hand upon me, saying unto me, 'Fear not; I am the First and the Last; I am He that liveth, and was dead; and, behold, I am alive for evermore, Amen; and have the keys of hell and of death.'" (Revelation 1:17-18)

The expression, "I am He that liveth, and was dead; and, behold, I am alive for evermore, shows us that the Lord Jesus is the Speaker, as this is a direct reference to His death and resurrection. However, the title, *The First and the Last*, reveals to us that the Speaker is also fully Divine, for this is a title of God HimSelf as we learn from Isaiah 41:4, "I the Lord (*Jehovah*), *the First, and with the Last;* I (*Jehovah*) am He." We may conclude that Christ, by appropriating to HimSelf the title that pertains to Jehovah in Isaiah 41:4, urges us to recognize that He HimSelf is the very same Person as Jehovah. Having seen that it is Christ Who is the Speaker in verses 17 & 18, Who names HimSelf *The First and the Last*, it necessarily follows that Christ is also the Speaker in verse 11, as it was the Author of these words, Who in fact claims the same title, "I am the Alpha and Omega, the First and the Last", Who first attracted John's attention, and caused him to turn around to see Who was speaking. (See verse

───────────────

and Omega, the Beginning and the End, the First and the Last", which the *R.S.V., Moffat,* and the *N.I.V.* all include. If the reader's own Bible does not have the words "Alpha and Omega" at chapter 1:11, they will probably be found at chapter 22:13.

12, then read on to verse 18). Here in verse 11, we find another title, *Alpha and Omega*, which agrees very well with the title, *First and the Last*, as *Alpha* and *Omega* are the first and last letters of the Greek alphabet, the language of the New Testament. What is particularly interesting about the appellation *Alpha and Omega* though, is that while it is applied to Christ in verse 11, in verse 8 it is applied to Almighty God. "*I am Alpha and Omega, the Beginning and the Ending saith the Lord, which is, and which was, and which is to come, the Almighty.*"

It is evident from the use of the term *Almighty*, that in verse 8, the title "Alpha and Omega, the Beginning and the Ending" (only a variant of *The First and the Last*) is applied to God, yet this title is the same as is given to the Speaker in verse 11, "I am Alpha and Omega, the First and the Last", therefore the Author of these words must also be God. However, the Speaker in verse 11, is the same Person as the Speaker in verses 17 & 18, as when John heard the words of verse 11, *he turned around to see the Speaker of verses 17 &18,* at Whose feet he then collapsed.

The use of the phrase, "I am the First and the Last", in verse 17, shows that the Speaker is the same as in verse 11. Comparing verses 11 & 8, shows us that this Person is God, yet the words, *uttered by the same Person,* "I am He that liveth, and was dead; and, behold, I am alive for evermore", referring as it does to the Passion of Jesus, means that *Christ alone* may be the Author of these words, and identifies Him, as being the Possessor of the titles, *Alpha and Omega,* and, *The First and the Last,* which Revelation 1:8 and Isaiah 41:4 show belong to Almighty God, or The Eternal One, Jehovah. It is my firm belief that we can only truly understand this passage of Scripture if we acknowledge the full Deity of our Lord and Saviour, Jesus Christ.[21]

The experience of John, on the Isle of Patmos, helps to explain to us the vision of God, which Isaiah received and recorded in chapter 6 of his book, which otherwise would be a puzzle to us. Isaiah says he saw, "The Lord sitting upon a throne, high and lifted up, and His train filled the Temple," (Isaiah 6:1). Now the Bible says clearly in 1 John 4:12 that, "No man hath seen God *at any time*", (cf. 1 Timothy 6:16) yet Isaiah states emphatically, "Mine eyes have seen the King, *Jehovah* of Hosts," (Isaiah 1:5 end). How can we resolve this seeming contradiction?

John again says in chapter 1, verse 18 of his Gospel, "No man hath seen God at any time:' but then goes on to tell us that, "the Only-Begotten Son, which is in the bosom of the Father, He hath declared Him."[22] Taking this together with the words of Jesus to Philip, "He that hath seen Me hath seen the Father," (John 14:9) we find a clue. Hebrews 1:3 assures us that Christ Jesus is "the Express Image" of God, "the Brightness (cf. Revelation 1:17, Matthew 17:2 & 2 Thessalonians 2:8) of His glory." Colossians 1:15 shows us that Christ is, "the *Image* of the *invisible* God." From all this we have learned that God the Father, is invisible, unseen, but that the

---

[21] *The Almighty* is a title which all recognize as belonging to God. In Revelation 1:8 *The Almighty* is said to be the One "Which is, and which was, and which is to come." This last clause, "which is to come," is in the Greek *Ho erchomenos,* and means literally, *the Coming One,* i.e. Christ! Hence Christ HimSelf is named *Almighty*, showing the equality of Christ and the Father.

[22] "The Only-Begotten Son" is in the Greek text according to Nestle *Ho monogenes Theos,* "The Only-Begotten *GOD"!*

Son has *declared* Him. He Who is *God-with-us*, is the image or *picture* of God. He is *God-made-visible*, (cf John 14:9 & Colossians 1:15). We see the Father by looking at the Son. The vision which Isaiah had of the *invisible* God could only be the *Image* of His Son Jesus, as with John in Patmos, for, "No man hath seen God at any time;" but, "the Only-Begotten Son, which is in the bosom of the Father, He hath declared Him," (John 1:18). This further evidence of Christ's Deity resolves what would otherwise be a contradiction in God's Word.

If we turn again to the book of Zechariah, we will find that Christ is directly referred to as Jehovah. In Zechariah 2:10, we read of the time of the Second Coming of Christ. "Sing and rejoice, O daughter of Zion: for, lo I come, and I will dwell in the midst of thee," saith the Lord (*Jehovah*). As we continue into verse 11, it is important to remember that the Speaker has been identified as *Jehovah*, (end of verse 10). "And many nations shall be joined to the Lord (*Jehovah*) in that day, and shall be My (*Jehovah's*) people: and I (*Jehovah*) will dwell in the midst of thee, and thou shalt know that the Lord (*Jehovah*) of Hosts hath sent Me (*Jehovah*) unto thee."

Now here we have *Jehovah* sending forth *Jehovah!* "Many nations shall be joined to *Jehovah* in that day, and shall be My (*Jehovah's*) people ... and thou shalt know that *Jehovah*...hath sent Me (*Jehovah*) unto thee." Here are two distinct Persons, called by the same Name of *Jehovah*. These Persons may only be Jehovah, the Father, sending forth His *Express Image* (cf Hebrews 1:3) Jehovah, the Word.

Turning now to Zechariah 3:2, we find a similar situation, "And the Lord (*Jehovah*) said unto Satan, 'The Lord (*Jehovah*) rebuke thee, O Satan; even the Lord (*Jehovah*) that hath chosen Jerusalem rebuke thee.'" Here, *Jehovah*, the Word, calls upon *Jehovah* the Father, to rebuke Satan, again displaying the existence of two Persons, each Named *Jehovah*.

These two Scriptures show with the utmost clarity that there exists within the Godhead more than one Being, called by the sacred Name of *Jehovah*. Two Divine Persons are beheld in these verses, and no longer may we believe that there is a *solitary* Person of *Jehovah*.

If we continue, we will find that there are other Scriptures that may be called upon for support in this respect. Genesis 19:24 records the destruction of Sodom and Gomorrah in the following words, "Then the Lord (*Jehovah*) rained upon Sodom and Gomorrah brimstone and fire from the Lord (*Jehovah*) out of Heaven." *Jehovah* brings down to the earth judgment from *Jehovah* in Heaven. The Father, and the Son co-operate in the overthrow of Sodom and Gomorrah, and Both bear the Name *Jehovah*.

If we turn to Judges 6:12, we find the following, "And the Angel of the Lord (*Jehovah*) appeared unto him (Gideon), and said unto him, 'The Lord (*Jehovah*) is with thee, thou mighty man of valour.'" Jehovah sends forth His Angel with the simple, but heartening message, "I am with you." Gideon expresses his doubts about this in verse 13, while in verse 14 we learn of the Angel's response. However, now the Angel HimSelf is named *Jehovah*, "And the Lord (*Jehovah*) (that is the Angel!) looked upon him, and said, 'Go in this thy might, and thou shalt save Israel from the hand of the Midianites: have not *I* sent thee?'" The same situation is found in verse 16, "And the Lord (*Jehovah*) (the Angel of verse 12) said unto him, 'Surely *I* will be with thee, and thou shalt smite the Midianites as one man.'"

Verses 20-24 make it plain that the Speaker was still the Angel, thus we find that Both the Angel, and the Lord Who sent Him, are named Jehovah.[23]

From this, the question immediately arises, "who is this Person, referred to as *The Angel of the Lord?*" The answer to this is again found in the Book of Judges, at chapter 13, verse 18. The Angel of the Lord had appeared to Manoah, who had asked Him, "What is Thy Name, that when Thy sayings come to pass we may do Thee honour?" (verse 17 cf John 13:19). The Angel replied, "Why askest

---

[23] Two further illustrations may be given to show that The Angel Of The Lord is Divine. Firstly, Genesis 16:7-13. Hagar, Sarai's handmaid, had run away from her mistress and was making for her native Egypt, when the Angel of the Lord appeared to her. After instructing Hagar to return to Sarai, the Angel said to her, "I will multiply thy seed exceedingly, that it shall not be numbered for multitude." Clearly this was no ordinary Angel, for He said that He, not the Lord, would multiply her seed, hence Hagar in verse 13 calls Him God, and Moses, the inspired writer of Genesis, in the same verse calls Him *Jehovah*, "And she called the Name of the Lord (*Jehovah*) (the Angel) that spake unto her, "Thou *God* seest me.' "

Secondly, Genesis 32:24-30. Jacob was returning to Canaan and had left himself alone on the plains at night where he encountered a Being Who wrestled with him until dawn approached. After his ordeal he realized that he had met with the Lord, for he said in verse 30, "I have seen God face to face, and my life is preserved." Hosea, when referring to this episode in Jacob's life, also calls Him *God* saying, "by his strength he had power with God: yea, he had power over the *Angel*, and prevailed," (Hosea 12:3-4). Here again the Angel is seen to be Divine.

The Fulness of the Godhead

thou thus after My Name, seeing it is *Wonderful?*" (Margin; also see *R.S.V.*). The Hebrew word translated *Wonderful* in Judges 13:18, is virtually identical to the word rendered *Wonderful* in Isaiah 9:6, where this Name is applied to Christ; they are both different forms of the Hebrew *Pala.* Isaiah 9:6 reads "For unto us a Child is born, unto us a Son is given: and the government shall be upon His shoulder: and His Name shall be called *Wonderful.*"[24] The Angel of the Lord is none other than the Word, the Son of God, significantly Named Jehovah, in Judges 6, as He is in Zechariah 2 and 3.

In his *Commentary on Genesis,* Derek Kidner has this to say on the subject of The Angel of the Lord, "We may note the occasional indications, in the terms, *the Angel of the Lord* or *of God* and *the Sprit of God,* that God's unity is not monolithic. A study of *the Angel of the Lord* passages leaves no room for doubt that **the term denotes God HimSelf** as seen in human form; what should be added is that *Angel* by its meaning *messenger,* implies that God, made visible, is at the same time God *sent.* In the Old Testament nothing is made of this paradox, but it should not surprise us that the apparent absurdity disappears in the New Testament. Just as *the Spirit of God* was an Old Testament expression awaiting its full disclosure at Pentecost, so *the Angel of the Lord,* as a term for the Lord HimSelf, becomes meaningful only in the light of 'Him Whom the Father … sent into the world', the pre-existent Son"[25] We may add that not only was Jesus *sent* (as an Angel being a messenger is sent) *from* God, but that He also came *out* (that is,

---

[24] See Strong's op.cit., under the entries for *wonderful & secret* and Gesenius op.cit., word Nos. 6382 & 6383.

[25] See *Genesis: An Introduction And Commentary* by Derek Kidner, pages 33-4, Tyndale Press.

became manifest) from God. (See John 16:27, 17:8, cf. 8:42 & 13:3).

Before leaving the subject of the Deity of Christ, we must first examine those verses of Scripture, which have on occasion been misunderstood by some who feel that they indicate that our Lord Jesus Christ is a *created* being.

The first verses we will look at are Revelation 3:14, where Christ is called "The Beginning of the creation of God," and Colossians 1:18 where He is again named, "The Beginning". Because Christ is addressed here as *The Beginning*, it is suggested that He is the very first creature that the Father ever made, and that because He was made, He is a *creature*, and not the *Creator*, so that He is less than God.

Now, the fact that God the Father is also named *The Beginning* in Revelation 1:8, shows us that this interpretation cannot be correct, as then it would necessarily mean that the Father also is a created being, and less than God, and that would leave us with the question, "Who created the Father?"!

The fact that *Both* the Father and the Son are called *The Beginning,* that it is a title they share, illustrates to us, not the *inferiority* of the Son, but the *equality* of the Son and the Father in being addressed by the same appellative. The Father is *The Beginning* inasmuch as He is *The Originator,* He is *The Source* of all creation. In the same way, John 1:1-3 and Colossians 1:16-17 show us that Christ is also *The Originator* or *Source* of the whole universe. All of creation was brought forth by Christ. If the term, *The Beginning,* meant that the Father and the Son were created, then the term *The Ending,* (Revelation 1:8), would mean that They will not always exist, that there would be a time when God was not. God is *The Beginning* by being *The Source* of our existence. He is *The Ending,* by being *The Goal* of our existence. These are terms by which the Infinite God relates to us, His finite creatures, they must not be construed as limitations of the Deity of either Father or Son.

The next text that we will consider is, "(Christ) Who is ...the *Firstborn* of every creature." Colossians 1:15. We have already observed that Christ is not a creature at all, but is instead, the Creator, so what does this scripture mean? To find the answer we have only to move on three verses, to verse 18, where we see the same expression, but this time with greater clarity. Christ is said to be, "the **Firstborn** *from the dead;* that in *all things* He might have the pre-eminence." The phrase "From the Dead" warns us that we are not to understand the term *Firstborn* chronologically.

The raising from the dead of the son of the widow of Zarephath by Elijah (1 Kings 17:17-23), and the raising by Christ HimSelf of the widow of Nain's son (Luke 7:11-15), Jairus' daughter (Luke 8:40-56) and Lazarus (John 11:38-44), as well as those who came forth from the graves at the time of Christ's Passion (Matthew 27:52-53), clearly demonstrate that Christ was far from being the *first* Person in Scripture to be raised from the dead. Indeed, the widow's son that Elijah raised preceded Christ by several centuries, yet the Bible categorically names the Lord Jesus, "The *Firstborn* from the dead," (Colossians 1:18), or "The *First Begotten* of the dead," (Revelation 1:5). The question now is, "May the term, *Firstborn,* be used in any other way?"

The answer is emphatically, "Yes!" In Jeremiah 31:9 the Lord said, "I am a Father to Israel, and Ephraim is My *Firstborn*." What is especially remarkable about this verse, is that Ephraim could not in any way be called *Firstborn* in a chronological sense. The founder of the tribe of Ephraim was the *younger* brother of Mannaseh who *was* the Firstborn, (Genesis 41:50-52). His father was Joseph, the oldest child of Rachel. However, Rachel was Jacob's *second* wife, and the *fourth* woman to bear him children. Further, the Scriptures show that Joseph was the eleventh child born to Jacob, and that Jacob himself was the *younger* of the twins born to Isaac and Rebekah. (See Genesis chapters 29 & 30, & 25:24-26). Neither Ephraim, nor his father, nor his father's father was *Firstborn,* so why does God call Ephraim by this title?

Returning to Ephraim's grandfather, Jacob (i.e. Israel: Genesis 32:28), we find that although younger than his brother Esau, God had determined to honour him as the *Firstborn,* (Genesis 25:23 end, cf. Romans 9:10-13). Jacob was the one whom God had chosen. Similarly, out of Jacob's twelve sons, it was the eleventh son, Joseph, whom God raised to a position of eminence over his brothers, (Genesis 37:5-10 & chapters 37:45). In the same way, with Joseph's own sons, the Lord had decreed that the younger Ephraim, not the older Mannaseh, was to be made the pre-eminent child, (Genesis 48:13-20). Thus, the tribe of Ephraim was named the Firstborn, *not* because its head and founder was literally the first child born to his father, but because of the position of pre-eminence which pertained to him.

Now, this is exactly what we find in Colossians 1:18. It is the *pre-eminence* of Christ that is emphasized by the terms *Firstborn.* Christ is named "the *Firstborn* from the dead", to show His superiority of position and authority, for His resurrection was greater by far than any of the instances cited earlier. It is the means of our salvation (1 Corinthians 15:17) and the sign that we shall also be raised from the grave, (2 Corinthians 4:14). The whole point of this verse is to show the eminence of Christ. He is declared to be, "the Head of the body ... *that in all things He might have the pre-eminence,"* (Colossians 1:18).

If it is objected that as verse 15 says of Christ He is the **"Firstborn** of *every creature*," this does not apply to the Resurrection but to the material creation, it should be remembered that Christ HimSelf used the same expression in Mark 16:15, "Preach the Gospel to *every creature*." Evidently this applies only to a *part* of the material creation, namely, mankind. As this is the case in Mark 16:15 why should it not be the case in Colossians 1:15, especially as it is explained as meaning just this in verse 18? Also in verse 23, where Paul says the Gospel was "preached to *every creature* which is under heaven," and at a time when very many were unevangelized.

Another common misunderstanding of the nature of the Word arises from the lowly and humble position He assumed when He became manifest as the Messiah, or the Christ, in the Person of Jesus. The Eternal Son allowed HimSelf to be "made in the likeness of men," (Philippians 2:7). The Divine Word of God, Who as "The Image of the Invisible God" (Colossians 1:15), or "God-made-visible", had appeared in human form in the days of the Old Testament as *The Angel of the Lord*, or, as *angel* means *messenger*, *God-sent*, became manifest by the Spirit in the womb of Mary, (Luke 1:30-35), the future wife of Joseph, as Jesus. The Express Image of God (Hebrews 1:3) was given substance, and made man, (Hebrews 2:9 & 10:5). The loveliness and nearness of God that pertained to *The Angel of the God* Who, as *God sent*, had appeared in the past to mankind, became real, substantial and lasting, in the glorious manifestation of *Emmanuel, God-with-us* (Matthew 1:23) in Jesus Christ, the Son of God, and the Son of Man.

Though He "thought it not robbery to be equal with God" (Philippians 2:6) He lowered HimSelf, to be born "of a woman, made under the Law" (Galatians 4:4). Though it is true that "in Him dwelleth all the fullness of the Godhead bodily" (Colossians 2:9) it is equally true that He became very man, (Philippians 2:7 & 1 John 4:2-3). Forsaking Eternity, He entered time and history. Forsaking Infinity, He entered the bounds of this world. Forsaking the glory He had with the Father, He took upon HimSelf our flesh. In His Person may be found God and man, the perfect Mediator of the Covenant, bringing God to man and man to God. (1 Timothy 2:5). Sadly though, the very Scriptures that show the real humanity of Christ, are thought by some to disprove His Divinity. What we must understand is that *both* natures co-exist within the One Person of Jesus Christ.

When He became man, He was as any other human being. He needed to eat, drink, and sleep as we all do. He needed to pray and worship. He had to develop mentally and spiritually, (Luke 2:52). In terms of His *humanity*, His knowledge was finite (Mark 13:32). In stooping to the human plane, He made no compromise, He asked for no concession, and though His Divinity unmistakably shone through His assumed humanity at times, as at the Transfiguration (Matthew 17:1-3), and in His discourses with the Jews (Mark 2:5-12 & John 5:18) and in His many Miracles of healing, increase of food, and even raising of the dead, He was also really and truly man.

This manhood necessitated His obedience to the Law, and submission to the Father. It is in *this* context that the words, "My Father is greater than I," (John 14:28) were uttered by Jesus, in the days of His *humiliation,* in the days of His *emptying* of HimSelf, when He took the form of a servant, and knew suffering and shame.

These words of Christ must not be used to tear from Him His Godhood, which we have clearly seen in the Scriptures we have already studied.

The humiliation of Christ is now no more. Now He is exalted in the Heavens (Hebrews 8:1). Possessor of all authority in the Heavens and the earth (Matthew 28:18), no longer having to submit to the earthly rules of the Romans and the Jews, as was the case when He said His Father was greater than Him. Now indeed, He had a Name *above* every other Name (Philippians 2:9) and *shares* His Father's throne, (Revelation 5:6). Once more our Lord Jesus Christ shares the glory He had with the Father before the world was, (John 17:5).

The humbling of Christ, for our sakes, should fill our hearts with wonder, and a feeling of unworthiness of so great a Love. At the same time, the realization that the Lord Jesus is firstly *God-made-visible*, secondly *God-sent*, and thirdly *God-with-us, Jehovah-our-righteousness,* should make Him unspeakably precious to us all, the "pearl of Great Price, for which a man gives his all, that he might possess it". (Colossians 1:15; John 8:42; 13:3, 16:27, 17:8; Isaiah 7:14; Matthew 1:23; Jeremiah 23:6; Matthew 13:45-46).

The Deity of Christ is something on which all believers depend, for, if Christ is not Divine, He cannot Mediate between God and man. Consider that between God and the most exalted creature He has made there is a veritable chasm. No mere creature can bring us to God. Christ can only draw us as close to God as He is HimSelf, which, if He was a creature, would be of no advantage to us. Finiteness can never approach infinity. In short, if Christ is not God, we are lost. Let us give thanks, that He is truly Divine; that He can save! Praise Him!

CONCLUSION

CONCLUSION

In the preceding pages much time and space has been devoted to searching the Scriptures in order to understand what Divine Revelation says of the Holy Spirit, and the Word, and of Their relationship with the Father. We must now see what conclusions may be drawn from that we have gathered.

At the start of this study, we noted that the Bible reveals that both the Spirit and the Word acted together with the Father in the mighty work of creation. We observed also how as Adam was about to be created, God spoke in a plural manner, saying, "Let *Us* make man in *Our* Image, after *Our* Likeness," (Genesis 1:260.

The Godhood of the Father was held to be universally acknowledged, but an examination of the Holy Spirit, and the Word of God, was deemed to be needful. Turning first to the Holy Spirit, we saw that the Scriptures show clearly that the Spirit is a real Person, and, further, that the attributes of Deity are accredited to Him by the Bible, and lastly we learned that He is called by the Sacred Name of Jehovah.

We then considered the Word, the Lord Jesus Christ. We found Him to be worshipped as God, to be invested with the Names and Titles of Deity, including, as with the Holy Spirit, the Name of Jehovah.

The knowledge that the Father, son and Spirit are All Named Jehovah, that they are All said by Scripture to be eternal, and All named as Creator, inevitably leads us to believe, as the Scriptures are insistent, that there is only One God, that the Only Living and

True God, Who said, "Let *Us* make," consists of a plurality of Persons. This doctrine is, I believe, at the heart of Deuteronomy 6:4, "Hear, O Israel: The Lord our God the Lord is one," (in the Hebrew order), as Dr. Bullinger shows very clearly. He writes of this text, "This fixes the doctrine of the Trinity. For the three Persons are named, and then it is declared that they are *one*: 'The Lord, our God, The Lord, is one,' *i.e.* the three, *Father, Son* and *Spirit,* are one."[26]

This is *not* to say that we believe in three gods! For we believe in only One God, Who is made known to us in three distinct Persons. While Each of These three Persons is fully Divine, completely Self-Existent, and Named Jehovah, no One of Them, Individually, comprises the Totality of the revealed Godhead.

Now, the Name Jehovah is, I believe, used to designate any One Person of the Godhead, Individually. However, for reasons I have set out in Appendix 1, I consider All three Members of the Godhead are included in the regular Name of God in Hebrew, *Elohim,* which is a plural word, although it is used in a singular sense.

Realizing that the Names of God are sometimes to be understood as embracing All the Persons of Deity, and on other occasions, only One Individual Member of the Godhead would, I suggest, prevent a great deal of misunderstanding over John 1:1, "In the beginning was the Word, and Word was with God, and the Word was God." This verse, I believe, shows Christ as the Word in union with the Father and the Spirit from eternity and, I propose, may be paraphrased thus: "In the beginning was the Word, and the Word

---

[26] *Number In Scripture,* by E.W. Bullinger, D.D., page 55, Kregel Publications.

was One of the Godhead, the Word was Divine," (For a discussion on John 1:1, please refer to Appendix 3).

The intimacy of the Union of Father, Son, and Spirit suggested by John 1:1 is beyond our understanding, yet we may appreciate some small degree of it from John 10:30, "I (Christ) and My Father are One," and John 10:38, "Believe that the Father is in Me, and I in Him."

There is a beauty in these sublime statements that transcends all human experience. The closeness of Father, Son, and Holy Spirit, may again be observed at the baptism of Christ, "and Jesus, when He was baptized, went up straightway out of the water; and, lo, the heavens were opened unto Him, and He saw the Spirit of God descending like a dove, and lighting upon Him: And lo a voice from heaven, saying, "This is My Beloved Son, in Whom I am well pleased,'" (Matthew 3:16-17).

The Father, Son and Spirit, All participated in the baptism, hence Jesus in Matthew 28·19 commanded His followers to be baptized, "In the Name of the Father, and of the Son, and of the Holy Ghost," Interestingly, in this verse we see All three Members of the Godhead sharing *one* Name. ("The Name", not "the Names".) We have then a Monotheism, not with the emptiness of Unitarianism, but with the richness or fullness of the Godhead (Colossians 2:9) of Father, Son and Spirit.

Paul concluded the second epistle to the Corinthians with a prayer which is very fitting for us to use at the close of this study. It is my prayer that these words may be true for all who read them. "The grace of the Lord Jesus Christ, and the love of God, and the communion of the Holy Ghost, be with you all," (2 Corinthians 13:14.)

Appendix 1:
ELOHIM

Appendix 1: ELOHIM

The Hebrews Name for God, *Elohim*, which means *The Mighty One,* is a *plural* word, though it is used in a *singular* sense.[27] The plurality of the word is indicated by the suffix, *'im'.*[28] We may observe the same suffix in *dabarim,* Hebrew for words, the plural of *dabar,* Hebrew for word, and in *goyim,* Hebrew for the gentile peoples, the plural of *goy,* Hebrew for an individual Gentile.[29]

Now, the word *God* occurs about 3,040 times in the *Authorized Version* of the Old Testament, and approximately 2,300 times it is translated from *Elohim,* which is a quite remarkable fact. It means that the plural Name for God is to be found *throughout* the Old Testament, being woven by the Holy Spirit into its very fabric, from Genesis to Malachi. The question we need to ask is, "What is the significance of the Bible using a plural Name for our God?"

The speculations that some of the more liberal-minded have made, that the use of the plural *Elohim* stems from polytheism, may be

---

[27] See Strong's *Exhaustive Concordance Of The Bible* & Young's *Analytical Concordance To The Holy Bible* & word No. 433 in Gesenius' *Hebrew & Chaldee Lexicon* & page xxvi of Davidson's *Analytical Hebrew & Chaldee Lexicon.*

[28] See *An Introductory Hebrew Grammar* by Davidson, page 55, T & T Clark.

[29] See word Nos. 1471 & 1697 of Gesenius op.cit., & pages cxliv & cxxxiii of Davidson's Lexicon op. cit.

safely ignored. It is hardly necessary to state that the God of the Bible owes nothing to the mumbo-jumbo of heathenism. Romans 1:18-25 shows that polytheism represented a *departure* from the original faith of man in One God. The truth is that Monotheism *predates* polytheism. When the tide of polytheism swept over the nations, it was the Monotheistic faith of the patriarchs that stood as a bastion against it. That the Divinely-inspired sacred Scriptures contain any hint of the error they so unequivocally witnessed against is inconceivable.

Indeed, the Holy Spirit introduced a safeguard against polytheism, by ensuring that the verbs used alongside the plural *Elohim* were (when applied to the True God) in the *singular* form. This created a unique style of grammar, which may be expressed as *plurality-in-the-singular,* or, as some refer to it, *uni-plurality*.

It is my conviction that these are matters that the Lord urges us to take notice of. Dr. P. Smith comments, "The fact which principally requires our attention, is the constant use of *Elohim*, to designate the one and only God. It is not a little remarkable that, in the sacred books of a people who were separated from all other nations for this express object, viz. that they should bear a public and continual protest against polytheism – the ordinary name and style of the only living and true God should be in a plural form. Did some strange and insuperable necessity lie in the way? Was the language so poor that it could furnish no other term? Or, if so, could not the wisdom of inspiration have suggested a new appellative, and for ever abolish the hazardous word? None of these reasons existed. The language was rich and copious. Besides 'that glorious and fearful name, *Jehovah,*' the appropriated and unique style of the true God, there was the *singular* form *'Eloah'* of the very word in question."[30]

Polytheism, then, does not hold the answer to the Scriptures' designation of our God by a plural Name. Then what does unravel this problem for us? How are we to understand it?

A solution that has attracted many, is to appeal to the *plural of majesty,* or more technically, the *pluralis majestaticus,* to explain why God uses plurals of HimSelf. God is not only a great King, but the King of kings, the Lord of all creation. Is it not to be expected that He would speak as our kings and queens do, in the plural number?

This view does find some support among the many authorities who have investigated the matter, Indeed the Hebrew word for *master* is found in the plural form, *adonim,* (e.g. Genesis 24:9 & 51, 39:19-20), which does seem to give credence to this suggestion. However, there are difficulties involved in holding to this belief. The ancient Canaanites are believed to have addressed their god in the royal manner, using a plural name[31] and I feel we have to beware, lest we introduce into the Scriptures pagan customs and ideas which find no support in the Bible.

It is to my mind noteworthy that the practice of speaking in the plural number is found nowhere in the Word of God. All the monarchs mentioned in the Scriptures speak in the singular number

---

[30] Quoted by E.H. Bickersteth in *The Trinity* pages 144-6 footnote, Kregel Publications.

[31] See A.H. Strong, *Systematic Theology* page 318, Pickering & Inglis.

as the examples in Genesis 12:18-19, 20:15-16, 2 Samuel 3:28, 1 Chronicles 12:17, Ezra 6:8, & 7:21 show. Those who support this view must needs go outside Divine Revelation, to *The Apocrypha,* to 1 Maccabees 10:19 & 11:31 to illustrate this principle. Further, if the use of the plural *Elohim* is a *pluralis majestaticus* then we would expect to find it used with a plural verb, as in modern-day instances, but this is not the case.

As an example, let us say that a member of England's Royal Family is speaking. He or she may well say, "we are" in place of "I am." However, as *Elohim* is used with a *singular* verb, this would result, in the case of our example above, in the expression "we am!"; obviously different from any normal grammatical structure.

Gesenius, in his *Hebrew Grammar* considers the question of *royal usage* and is of the opinion that "the plural used by God in Gn 1:26, 11:7, Is 6:8, has been incorrectly explained in this way," (i.e. as a *pluralis majestaticus*). He concludes that, "The use of the plural as a form of respectful address is quite foreign to Hebrew,"[32] A.H. Strong says of *Elohim*, "Nor is it sufficient to call this plural a simple *pluralis majestaticus;* since it is easier to derive this common figure from Divine usage than to derive the Divine usage from this common figure,"[33]

Delitzsch, and Von Rad both adopt the classical Jewish view that the plural personal pronouns of Genesis 1:26, 11:7, & Isaiah 6:8, are to be understood as embracing the angelic hosts together with the Lord. However, this, in the case of Genesis 1:26, is coming very

---

[32] Gesenius' *Hebrew Grammar* section 124, subsection G pages 398-9, Oxford, The Clarendon Press.
[33] A.H. Strong page 318, op.cit.

close to attributing specific creative acts to the angels, and as Matthew Poole observes, "The angels rejoiced at the work of creation, but only God wrought it, (Job 38:4-7)".[34] Delitzch proposes that it was the angels' sympathy that God was seeking, but even this seems to clash with Isaiah 40:14, "With whom took He counsel?", and gives what S.R. Driver calls, "a strained limitation of the expression."[35]

I believe a more probable explanation for using a plural Name for God is that He is a Being Who is to be worshipped for a *multitude* of reasons. Every one of God's manifold attributes should summon forth pure adoration from our hearts, and the belief that the use of a plural form is to intensify, or enhance the meaning of the singular *Eloah* is well supported.

The Hebrew word for *master* is often found in the plural, as we have already noted, for this very reason. Both Davidson and Driver, among others, uphold this interpretation. Davidson is of the view that *Elohim* expresses, "a plenitude of might,"[36] while Driver says it is "indicative ... of the fullness of attributes and powers conceived as united in the Godhead."[37] But, is this all that may be said of *Elohim?* Or is there more for us to uncover?

---

[34] Matthew Poole, *A Commentary On The Whole Bible,* notes on Genesis 1:26, Banner Of Truth.

[35] See S.R. Driver, *The Book Of Genesis,* notes on Genesis 1:26, page 14, Westminster Commentaries, Methuen.

[36] Davidson, *The Theology Of The Old Testament,* chapter 3, section 3, *The unity of God,* page 100. International Theological Library, T & T Clark.

[37] Driver, op.cit. (page 14).

It is my conviction that just as every Name given to the Lord in the Bible is descriptive of Him in one way or another, and teaches us something about His nature, so the *form* of the Name *Elohim,* that of *plurality,* is descriptive of the plurality that exists in God. I believe the use of *Elohim* teaches us something about God's very Being. The plurality of *Elohim* does not urge us to believe in more than one god, because, although it is a plural word, it is used in a *singular* sense, and with a *singular* verb, as we have seen.

The combination of plurality and singularity that pertains to *Elohim*, to me, is highly suggestive of the *plurality* of Persons in the One and Only, or *Singular* True God. A purely singular, or a purely plural term, could never convey to us at once these two facets of our God, and indicates to me why the term was originally selected.

A.H. Strong remarks, "When finite things were pluralized to express man's reverence, it would be far more natural to pluralize the Name of God. And God's purpose in securing this pluralization may have been more far-reaching and intelligent that man's. The Holy Spirit Who presided over the development of revelation may well have directed the use of the plural in general, and even the adoption of the plural name *Elohim* in particular, with a view to the future unfolding of truth with regard to the Trinity."[38]

Both Davidson and Driver are opposed to seeing any connection between the plurality of Persons in the Godhead, and the use of plurals by God in the Scriptures, but others are not so inclined.

---

[38] A.H. Strong page 319 op.cit.

Matthew Henry, in his *Commentary of the Bible*, says that the Name *Elohim*, "Bespeaks... The plurality of Persons in the Godhead, Father Son and Holy Ghost. This plural name of God, in Hebrew, which speaks of Him as many, though He is One ... is to us a savour of life unto life, confirming our faith in the doctrine of the Trinity, which, though but darkly in the Old Testament, is clearly revealed in the New,"[39] E.H. Bickersteth in *The Trinity* says, "I should be doing injustice to my own conviction if I did not state, that I believe this language (the plurals; Us, Our, and *Elohim*,) was intended to foster when kindled, and to awaken when dormant, the persuasion that there subsisted a plurality in the essential unity of Jehovah."[40]

Remarking on the same plurals, Gesenius says they are, 'best explained as a plural of Self-deliberation."[41] The Rev. Derek Kidner believes that they represent, "the plural of fullness, which is found in the regular word for God (*Elohim*) used with a singular verb; and this fullness, glimpsed in the Old Testament, was to be unfolded as tri-unity, in the further 'we' and 'our' of John 14:23 (with 14:17)."[42] A.H. Strong observes, "The fact that *Elohim* is sometimes used in a narrower sense, as applicable to the Son (Psalm 45:6, cf. Hebrews 1:8), need not prevent us from believing that the term was originally chosen as containing an allusion to a certain plurality in the divine nature." [43]

---

[39] Matthew Henry *An Exposition Of The Old And New Testaments* notes on Genesis 1:1 Samuel Bagster, London.

[40] E.H. Bickersteth, page 145 footnote op.cit.

[41] Gesenius, Section 124, subsection G pages 398-9 op.cit.

[42] The Rev. Derek Kidner, *Genesis An Introduction And Commentary* pages 51-2 The Tyndale Press.

[43] A.H. Strong, page 318, op.cit.

So far we have considered *Elohim* in isolation from any other Name of God. However, in Genesis 2:4, it is found together with the Name *Jehovah,* and is translated by the *Authorized Version* as *The Lord God.* We must now ask, "does the singular Name *Jehovah* or *Yahweh* in any way qualify the plural *Elohim*?"

It has been suggested that the correct rendering of *Jehovah-Elohim* is *Jehovah-God,* which implies that only One Person, Who is referred to as *Jehovah,* comprises the Deity. This, of course, has important bearings on our understanding of the Name *Elohim,* so it is right that we should examine this phrase.

Now, The Name *Jehovah* is rendered both *God* and *Lord* in the *Authorized Version*, which is a little strange, as there is another word for *God (Elohim)* and another word for *Lord (Adonay),* *Jehovah* means *Self-Existent* or *Eternal-One,*[44] and perhaps this

---

[44] Ibid, page 257, & Gesenius op.cit. word No. 3068. It is particularly interesting that Gesenius compares the explanation of the meaning of *YHWH* given in Exodus 3:14, which he gives as being "I (ever) shall be (the same) that I am (to-day)," with the text of Revelation 1:4 & 8, *"Ho on kai ho en kai ho erchomenos."* Who is, Who was, and Who is to come, or more accurately, The Coming One." (Christ; see note 10 of Section 3 *The Lord Jesus Christ.)* Corroboration for this has been sought by numerous commentators by comparing Exodus 3:14, "Say unto the children of Israel, *I AM* hath sent me," with the seven "I Am's of Christ, in John 6:35,41,48,51, (I am the Bread of Life); 8:12 & 9:5, (I am the Light of the world); 10:7,9, (I am the Door); 10:11,14, (I am the Good Shepherd); 11:25, (I am the Resurrection and the Life); 14:6, (I am

would have been a preferable rendering, but often it would have been better left untranslated as *YHWH,* or *Yahweh,* or the anglicized *Jehovah.*

Now what can *Jehovah,* when used alongside *Elohim,* reveal to us? *Jehovah* and *Elohim* are both Names and, therefore, both nouns, and this is a help to us, because when two nouns are placed in apposition, one of them must become an adjective. This is a basic law of grammar. What needs to be established here is … which of the two nouns becomes the adjective.

James Moffat translates *Jehovah-Elohim, God the Eternal,* making *Jehovah (The Eternal One)* qualify or describe *Elohim (God).* However, I believe that there is an alternative to this rendering. In Hebrew, unlike English, it is usual for the adjective of relation (frequently called 'demonstrative') to come second, that is, *after* the noun. This fact inclines me to believe that the preferable rendering of *Jehovah-Elohim* is *The Divine Jehovah.* This would make the second noun *Elohim* become the adjective, and to my mind would be more consistent with Hebrew usage.

The difference between *Jehovah-God* and *The Divine Jehovah* may seem trifling and unimportant. However, the significance is that the expression *The Divine Jehovah* allows the existence of more Persons than one in the Godhead, which the less accurate *Jehovah-God* does not. The plural *Elohim,* already established in Genesis chapter 1 as pertaining to the Creator Who said, "Let *Us* make man in *Our* Image," (verse 26), shows that *Jehovah,* now Named for

---

the Way, the Truth, and the Life); 15:1,5,, (I am the True Vine). And also in comparing the meaning of *YHWH* with Hebrews 13:8 "Jesus Christ the same yesterday, and today, and for ever."

the first time, is a Divine Person or "One of Us" (Genesis 3:22), but importantly permits also the existence of other Divine Persons.

The Name *Jehovah* leads us to a further consideration. The most well-known and oft repeated passage in the Old Testament which mentions the Name *Jehovah,* is seen as the very bedrock on which the doctrine of Monotheism is founded. The Shema of Deuteronomy 6:4, "Hear, O Israel; The Lord our God is one Lord," is recited as a daily prayer by faithful Jews (Mark 12:29). Can the view of *Elohim* I am advocating be reconciled to the teaching of this verse? Let us look at the text itself, and do all we can to discover its meaning.

The crucial word *one* is translated from the Hebrew word *echad,* the same word that is rendered *one* in Genesis 2:24, "Therefore shall a man leave his father and his mother, and shall cleave unto his wife; and they shall be one *(echad)* flesh." Now here we have two separate and distinct persons said to be *one,* showing us that the word *echad (one)* may legitimately be used with a plurality of persons. The same word is found again in Genesis 11:6, where the Lord said, "Behold, the people is *one (echad).* "[45] Now it would be obviously mistaken to say that there was only one person alive in the whole world at that time! But if we say that the word *echad* can refer only to a *numeric* value of *one,* then this is the situation we find ourselves in! Clearly, some other meaning is intended.

If we look at the word *echad* we find it means a *unity,* and comes from the verb *achad,* which means to *unify* or *collect together.* Thus, Moses could speak of Adam and Eve as being *one* inasmuch as they were *united* in marriage. So also could he record in Genesis

---

[45] See Strong's Concordance op.cit.

11 that the people were *one* because they were *collected together,* (see verse 4b).[46] Now what is true of Genesis 2:24 & 11:6, is also true of Deuteronomy 6:4. It is precisely the same word that Moses used, *echad, a unity,* permitting a plurality of Persons, enabling the text to be read more clearly, thus: "Hear, O Israel: The Lord our God is a *United* or *Unified* Lord."

Dr. P Smith says about this verse, "Had it been intended to assert such a unity in the Divine nature, as is absolutely solitary, and exclusive of every modification of plurality, would not the expression of necessity have been this, "Hear, O Israel, *Jehovah, our Elohim, one Eloah"?* But, as the words actually stand, they appear to be in the most definite and expressive manner designed to convey the idea, that, *notwithstanding* a real plurality intimated in the form *Elohim, Jehovah* is still ONE."[47]

E.W. Bullinger makes some interesting remarks on the Shema in his book, *Number In Scripture.* He writes, "The Hebrew words may be variously rendered, but the quotation of the Lord Jesus, written by the Holy Spirit in the Gospels, fixes the meaning of the words. In the Hebrew the order is, 'Hear, O Israel, Jehovah our Elohim, Jehovah One,' The Jews repeat it to-day thus, 'Hear, O Israel, the Lord our God, the Lord is One,' and the whole congregation repeat the word 'One' for several minutes." (Footnote: "As *Elohim* is plural we might with much more reason repeat *Elohenu* for several minutes!")

If the Lord had not supplied the verb which fixes the meaning, we might well have read it as the Jews do, for this fixes (unconsciously

---

[46] Ibid.

[47] E.H. Bickersteth, op.cit. page 146; Footnote.

to them) the doctrine of the Trinity. For the three Persons are named, and then it is declared that they are *one:* "The Lord, our God, The Lord, is one," *i.e.* the three, *Father, Son and Spirit,* are *one.*

The real sense of the words, according to their meaning, is, "Hear, O Israel, *Jehovah* (the ever-existing One) our *Elohim* (our Triune God), *Jehovah* 'is one'."[48]

---

[48] See *Number In Scripture* by E.W. Bulliger, page 55, Kregel Publications. Dr. Bullinger gives a slightly different interpretation of the Shema two pages later, where he represents it as meaning, *Jehovah* (the Father), *Elohim* (the Son), and *Jehovah* (the Spirit) is *Echad:*-One Triune God," The Numerics of the text are quite intriguing. The numerical value of the sentence, "Hear, O Israel: The Lord our God is one Lord," is 1,118.

Hear	Shema	410
O Israel	Israel	541
The Lord	YHWH	26
Our God	Elohenu	102
The Lord	YHWH	26
Is One	Echad	13
		———
Total		1,118

This total is the product of 43 (which Ivan Panin discovered to be a number which features throughout the Scriptures. See his *Bible Chronology* Page 172 –part III section 27) & 26, which is the number of YHWH: 43x26= 1,118. It is also the product of 86 & 13; 86 x 13 = 1,118. 86 is the number of *Echad* (One). Thus the entire text, numerically, is the product of *Elohim* (God) & *Echad*

The Fulness of the Godhead   74

We may conclude therefore, that not only is there nothing about the use of *Elohim* that prevents us from regarding it as signifying the fullness of the Godhead that is revealed to us in the separate Persons of the Father, the Son, and the Spirit, but also that there are reasons for encouraging this belief.

For my part, I am grateful that this is so. If the Old Testament did not contain indications that God consisted of a plurality of Persons, which the New more clearly reveals to us, it would be less easy to demonstrate that the belief in the Deity of the Father, Son, and Spirit was not simply a device to reconcile disparate Theologies in the Two Testaments. I rejoice in the fact that it may be shown that both the Old and New are consistent in presenting us with a single Godhead, of a plurality of Persons. To my mind it is deeply significant that the Holy Spirit caused the Scriptures to record that God on occasion spoke in a plural manner, and that He was usually addressed by the plural form of the singular *Eloah*, which is akin to the Arabic Allah, the uncompromisingly Unitarian god of Islam. I praise God that the Unitarianism of the Koran is not to be found in the Bible, but, instead, Father, Son and Holy Spirit, the fullness of the Godhead. (Colossians 2:9).

(One), which encapsulates the gist of the whole verse "God (is) One." It also juxtaposes the two *uni-plural* words *Elohim* and *Echad*. The former being a plural word used in a singular manner, and the latter meaning a *compound unity* or, we could say, a singular made from a plurality. This encourages me to think that *Elohim* **IS** *Echad,* a compound unity, a plurality of Persons in One God.

The Fulness of the Godhead

Appendix 2:
JESUS IS LORD

Appendix 2:
JESUS IS LORD

1 Corinthians 12:3 says, "No man can say that Jesus is the Lord, but by the Holy Ghost." When we consider that Jesus HimSelf said in Matthew 7:21-23 that many whom He will *disown* will call Him, "Lord, Lord," it seems that what is important is what a person *means* by addressing Christ in this manner. Evidently it is possible to call Jesus "Lord" in a way which is purely superficial.

The Greek word *Kurios* (Lord) is the word used by the *Septuagint,* the Bible of the early Church, to translate the Sacred Name *YHWH.* The Jews became so fearful of taking the Name *YHWH* in vain, that they always spoke the word *Adonay* whenever they encountered *YHWH* in the Scriptures .*Kurios* is simply the Greek equivalent of the Hebrew *Adonay.*

Thus the early Christian confession, "Jesus is Lord" may be seen as a declaration that Jesus is *Adonay,* the One Whose Name was expressed by the tetragrammaton *YHWH.*

Now, of course, every *non*-believer is capable of actually uttering the word, "Lord", and of addressing Jesus in this way. However, non-believers have not the Spirit of God, and therefore, cannot Name Jesus "Lord", understanding by the Holy Spirit that the term denoted *Jehovah.* No man can say that Jesus is *Jehovah,* except he first receive revelation of that fact through the Holy Spirit ministering the Word of God to a Regenerated heart.

Appendix 3: JOHN CHAPTER 1 VERSE 1

Appendix 3:
JOHN CHAPTER 1
VERSE 1

The text of John 1:1 reads in the Greek as follows; *En arche en ho logos, kai ho logos en pros ton theon, kai theos en ho logos."* In the last clause, *"kai theos en ho logos"*, "and the Word was God", *Theos*, (God), does not have the definite article, which it does have in the second clause, *"kai ho logos en pros ton theon"*, "and the Word was with (the) God." The fact that Christ is called *Theos*, and not *Ho Theos* in this verse, is seen by some as evidence that He is less than God. This view, however, is unable to be sustained for very long, as later on in the same Gospel, Christ is clearly and distinctly addressed as *Ho Theos*. John 20:28, "Thomas answered and said unto Him (Jesus), 'My Lord and my God (*Ho Theos*).'"[49]

The absence of the article may readily be explained as no more than a Greek idiom. It has been pointed out by able Greek scholars that if a definite predicate noun precedes the verb (*theos & en* respectively in our case) then very often it does not have the article. This would indeed explain why the article is missing here.

---

[49] If Thomas was using the Name of God as an exclamation, as has been suggested, then unquestionably he would have broken the Third Commandment (Exodus 20:7). As Jesus did not utter one word of correction about his using the Divine Name, this cannot be the case.

However, I suspect that weightier considerations hold the real answer.

Ho Theos being the stronger term, I believe it refers to the *Totality* of the Godhead; the Union of Father, Son, and Spirit. This being so, the second clause of John 1:1 places Christ in the Godhead of *Ho Theos,* "and the Word was *with* God", or "and Christ was a Part of", or "a Member of", or "One of (cf Genesis 3:22) *Ho Theos.*" All three Members of the Godhead, Father, Son and Spirit, may be said to be "with *Ho Theos*" in this way, and Each Individual Person may thus be named *"Theos"*, a Part of *"Ho Theos"*. If One Member only of the Godhead was called in *this* passage *"Ho Theos"*, it would eliminate the Other Two Persons from the Godhead. Hence, if Christ was named here *"Ho Theos"*, Both the Father and the Holy Spirit would be *excluded* from the Deity! David J. Ellis says concerning John 1:1:

> The absence of the definite article in front of 'God', taken by some to mean that the Word possessed something less than full deity, implies, however, that other persons exist outside the second Person of the Trinity.[50]

Professor R.V.G. Tasker in his Commentary on John's Gospel states:

> In the original, there is no definite article before God. The significance of this is that the Word does not by Himself

---

[50] *A New Testament Commentary,* edited by G.C.D. Howley, F.F. Bruce, & H.L. Ellison, page 254, Pickering & Inglis.

make up the entire Godhead; nevertheless the divinity that belongs to the rest of the Godhead belongs also to Him.[51]

Andrew Miller discusses this verse in his *Church History,* and observes:

He (Christ) is here spoken of as the Word, the correlate of which is not the Father, but God (and thus leaving room for the Holy Spirit); but, lest His Own consubstantiality should be overlooked, He is carefully and at once declared to be God. (Footnote; The absence of the article here is necessarily due to the fact that *Theos* is the predicate of *ho logos*, in no way to an inferior sense of His Godhead, which would contradict the context itself, Indeed, if the article had been inserted, it would be the grossest heterodoxy, because its effect would be to deny that the Father and the Spirit are God by excluding all but the Word from Godhead.)[52]

Westcott remarks:

The predicate stands emphatically first. It is necessarily without the article, inasmuch as it describes the nature of the

[51] *John; An Introduction And Commentary,* by R.V.G. Tasker, page 45, Inter-Varsity Press.
[52] *Miller's Church History,* by Andrew Miller, page 1071, Pickering & Inglis.

Word and does not identify his person. It would be pure Sabellianism[53] to say: "The Word was *ho Theos*."[54]

Finally, Marcus Dods tells us:

> The Word is distinguishable from God, yet *Theos en ho logos* - the Word was God, of divine nature; not 'a God', which to a Jewish ear would have been abominable, nor yet identical

---

[53] Sabellius was a Presbyter who taught in Rome in the early 3rd. Century. He held that God had at first been a Monad, living in silence, and that He expanded to become a Trinity in process of time. God, as united to the creation, was the Father, as united to the Christ, He was the Son, and as united to the Church, He was the Spirit. He believed that in time to come God would again be reduced to a Monad. The Names, Father, Son and Spirit are but different and temporary manifestations of God, not real Persons.

This view of the Godhead is called by Theologians **Economic,** whereas the view most generally held to be orthodox is named **Necessary & Eternal.** What Sabellius did was to introduce change or evolution, not into the things God has made, or into His dealings with men, but into the very *Being* of God HimSelf. The Bible says that Jesus Christ is, "the same yesterday, and today, and for ever," (Hebrews 13:8). James writes of "the Father of lights, with Whom is no variableness," (James 1:17). Malachi 3:6 says "I am the Lord, I change not." The Economic view of Sabellius thus runs contrary to the Word of God, which demonstrates the Eternity of the Father (Romans 16:26), the Son (Isaiah 9:6) and the Spirit (Hebrews 9:14).

[54] Quoted in *Systematic Theology* by A.H. Strong, page 306, Pickering & Inglis.

with all that can be called God, for then the article would have been inserted.[55]

The glory which Christ had with the Father from the beginning (cf John 17:5) which is revealed to us by this verse, makes His humiliation for our sakes appear all the more remarkable, especially when we compare John 1:1 & 1:14. Though Christ "was God" (v.1) yet He was pleased to be "made flesh" (v.14). Though He was "with God' (v.1), He willingly "dwelt among us" (v.14). The love of Christ which led Him to do this is simply beyond description. "worthy is the Lamb that was slain to receive power, and riches, and wisdom, and strength, and honour, and glory, and blessing." (Revelation 5:12).

---

[55] Ibid.

ALSO ON THE GODHEAD

The Trinity in John

W M Henry

This book is a study of the relationships between the members of the Trinity and between the Trinity and Christian believers, focusing mainly on the Gospel of John.

The book opens with a discussion of the titles given to the Lord Jesus in John's Gospel and what they tell us about His relationship with His Father.

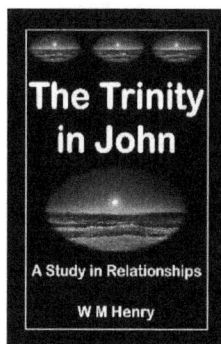

Section two explores the relationship between the Father and the Son and their joint work of redemption.

The book then widens the focus to examine the relationship between the Father, the Son and the believer before discussing the Holy Spirit and His relationship with other members of the Trinity, and with the believer.

Each chapter closes with brief meditative "Reflections" on the implications of the issues raised in the chapter. These are followed by suggestions for further study, which can be the basis for private devotions or group discussions.

The Fulness of the Godhead

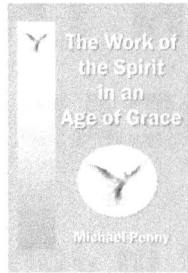

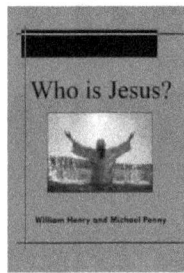

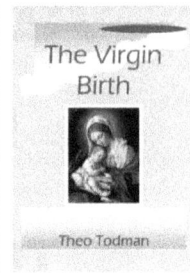

Jesus: God and Man
Brian Sherring

The Work of the Spirit in an Age of Grace
Michael Penny

Who is Jesus?
W M Henry and Michael Penny

The Virgin Birth
Theo Todman

The Deity of Christ
Vicky Wilkinson

Further details of the books on these pages, and the next, can be seen on

www.obt.org.uk

The books are available from that website and from

The Open Bible Trust
Fordland Mount, Upper Basildon,
Reading, RG8 8LU, UK.

They are also available as eBooks from Amazon and Apple, and as
KDP paperback from Amazon

FURTHER READING

The Miracles of the Apostles
Michael Penny

Why did the Apostles perform miracles?
Why were they able to perform them?
What was the purpose of the miracles?
What did they signify to the Jews?
Why did the Gentiles misunderstand them?
Why was Paul, later, not able to heal?
When did the miracles cease?
Why did they cease?

This book answers these questions, explains the significance and purpose of each type of miracle performed by the Apostles, and makes it clear why such miracles are not in evidence today.

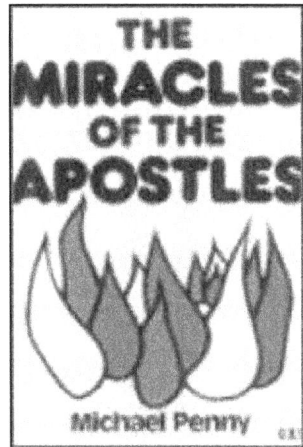

Salvation

Safe and Secure

Sylvia Penny

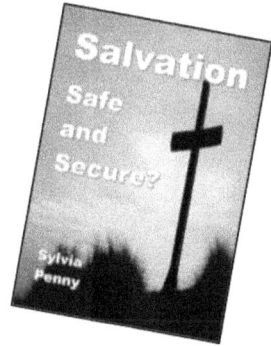

This important book is a
thorough treatment of the
subject of salvation, asking such
questions as …

- What is it, exactly, that saves us?
- Is salvation secure?
- Can it be lost?
- What is 'conditional security'?

It deals with a wide number of issues such as …

- Salvation and works
- The doctrine of rewards
- Lordship salvation
- Free grace theology
- Assurance of salvation
- Why people lose their faith

ABOUT THE AUTHOR

Michael Phelan was born in Harpenden, Hertfordshire in 1953. He trained as a photographer but deteriorating eyesight forced him to change direction, He then worked in the production control office of a light engineering company and lives in Southwick, near Brighton.

SEARCH MAGAZINE

For a free sample of
the Open Bible Trust's magazine *Search*,
please visit

www.obt.org.uk/search

or email

admin@obt.org.uk

ABOUT THIS BOOK

The Fulness of the Godhead

This publication will benefit greatly those who wish to understand what the Bible teaches concerning:

- The nature of the Lord Jesus Christ;
- The nature of the Holy Spirit;
- Their relationship to the Father.

Throughout the history of the Christian Church, men had asked whether Christ is truly God and have discussed whether the Holy Spirit is a real person or simply a Divine force.

This helpful publication provides the Bible's answers to those, and similar, questions.

Publications of The Open Bible Trust must be in accordance with its evangelical, fundamental and dispensational basis. However, beyond this minimum, writers are free to express whatever beliefs they may have as their own understanding, provided that the aim in so doing is to further the object of The Open Bible Trust. A copy of the doctrinal basis is available at

www.obt.org.uk/doctrinal-basis

or from:

THE OPEN BIBLE TRUST
Fordland Mount, Upper Basildon,
Reading, RG8 8LU, UK

www.ingramcontent.com/pod-product-compliance
Lightning Source LLC
Chambersburg PA
CBHW062114040426
42337CB00042B/2263